Now the music can begin.
These birds can really play!

Here's the long-necked emu.
She beats a big bass drum.

The turtle doves both play guitars.
They love to pick and strum.

The penguins all play tambourines.
They rattle and they bang.

4

The cuckoos play the cymbals,
and make them crash and clang.

5

The eagles play the trumpets.
These birds can really blow.

The owls blow on their bugles,
and swing them high and low.

Next come the pink flamingoes,
so elegant and tall.

With their big tubas they can make
the loudest noise of all!

The author would like to thank Janet Hillman for her contribution to this project.

Printed in Australia
ISBN 0 7327 1416 8

Published in the United States of America by
MIMOSA PUBLICATIONS
P.O. Box 26609
San Francisco CA 94126
(800) 443 7389

Published in the United Kingdom by
KINGSCOURT PUBLISHING
P.O. Box 1427
London W6 9BR
0800 317457

Published in Australia by
MIMOSA PUBLICATIONS
8 Yarra Street
Hawthorn
Victoria 3122

Kindergarten — Beginnings II — number groups